Source Books in
Landscape Architecture
5

Paolo Bürgi
Landscape Architect
Discovering the (Swiss) Horizon: Mountain, Lake, and Forest

Raffaella Fabiani Giannetto, Editor

Princeton Architectural Press, New York

SOURCE BOOKS IN ARCHITECTURE:

Morphosis/Diamond Ranch High School

The Light Construction Reader

Bernard Tschumi/Zénith de Rouen

UN Studio/Erasmus Bridge

Steven Holl/Simmons Hall

Mack Scogin Merrill Elam/Knowlton Hall

Zaha Hadid/BMW Central Building

Eisenman Architects/The University of Phoenix Stadium for the Arizona Cardinals

SOURCE BOOKS IN LANDSCAPE ARCHITECTURE:

Michael Van Valkenburgh/Allegheny Riverfront Park

Ken Smith Landscape Architect/Urban Projects

Peter Walker and Partners/Nasher Sculpture Center Garden

Grant Jones/Jones & Jones/ILARIS: The Puget Sound Plan

Paolo Bürgi Landscape Architect/Discovering the (Swiss) Horizon: Mountain, Lake, and Forest

Published by

Princeton Architectural Press

37 East Seventh Street

New York, New York 10003

For a free catalog of books, call 1.800.722.6657.

Visit our web site at www.papress.com.

Image credits:

All illustrations © Paolo Bürgi, unless otherwise noted.

Pages 11 top left and middle left, 11 bottom left and right, 12 top middle, 12 bottom left, 40, 42, 45, 46 top, 49, 56, 57 left, 58, 59 bottom, 61, 63 top left, 69 top, 70, 71 left, 92 top right, 94 bottom, 95, 97 right, 103, 109, 110: © Giosanna Crivelli

Pages 12 bottom right, 98, 101 left: © Thomas Gut

Pages 36, 38 bottom right: Drawings by Mei Wu

Pages 48 top, 55, 59 top, 71 right, 99 bottom, 107, 120: © Raffaella Fabiani Giannetto

Page 54 bottom: © Massimo Venturi Ferriolo

Pages 57 right, 80: © Stephan L. Bürgi

Pages 90, 114, 115: © Chiara Pradel

Pages 100 top, 112: © Dinah-Florentine Schmidt

Page 131: © Dilip da Cunha

Editor: Nicola Bednarek

Designer: Jan Haux

Layout: Bree Anne Apperley

Special thanks to: Nettie Aljian, Sara Bader, Janet Behning, Becca Casbon, Carina Cha, Penny (Yuen Pik) Chu, Carolyn Deuschle, Russell Fernandez, Pete Fitzpatrick, Wendy Fuller, Clare Jacobson, Aileen Kwun, Nancy Eklund Later, Linda Lee, Laurie Manfra, John Myers, Katharine Myers, Lauren Nelson Packard, Dan Simon, Andrew Stepanian, Jennifer Thompson, Paul Wagner, Joseph Weston, and Deb Wood of Princeton Architectural Press —Kevin C. Lippert, publisher

Library of Congress Cataloging-in-Publication Data:

Paolo Bürgi landscape architect : discovering the (Swiss) horizon : mountain, lake, and forest / Raffaella Fabiani Giannetto, editor. — 1st ed.

   p. cm. — (Source books in landscape architecture ; 5)

 Includes bibliographical references.

 ISBN 978-1-56898-851-1 (alk. paper)

1. Bürgi, Paolo—Interview. 2. Landscape architects—Switzerland—Interview.

3. Minimal architecture—Switzerland. 4. Landscape architecture—Philosophy.

I. Fabiani Giannetto, Raffaella.

SB469.386.S95P36 2009

712.092—dc22

                              2009014404

Contents

Acknowledgments

I met Paolo Bürgi at the University of Pennsylvania School of Design, where I took his landscape design studio as a master's student. This book is a way to express my deep gratitude for everything that he has taught me, in particular for his contagious enthusiasm for the craft of landscape architecture and for his inspiring dedication. I would also like to thank him for his gracious hospitality in Switzerland and for guiding me through the mystery and wonder of his projects.

In accepting my invitation to participate in the Glimcher seminars at the Ohio State University in the spring of 2005, Bürgi again proved to be a very generous professional and teacher. The seminars focused on an overview of his work, his design philosophy, and the many practical applications of his phenomenological approach to landscape architecture. The last days were spent on an in-depth analysis of the three projects presented in this book, namely, Cardada, Kreuzlingen Hafenplaz, and the Terrace on the Forest at Sementina.

I am grateful to the students who attended the seminars and helped transcribe the recordings, particularly Jake Boswell and Jackie Cmunt.

Many thanks also to John Dixon Hunt for his critical essay on Bürgi's work, and to Sonja Dümpelmann for her willingness to share her insights and for contributing to this volume. Finally, I am indebted to Chiara Pradel at Bürgi's office for helping me select the illustrative material, and to Nicola Bednarek, my editor at Princeton Architectural Press.

Raffaella Fabiani Giannetto

Source Books in Landscape Architecture

Source Books in Landscape Architecture provide concise investigations into contemporary designed landscapes by looking behind the curtain and beyond the script to trace intentionality and results. One goal is to offer unvarnished stories of place-making. A second goal is to catch emerging and established designers as facets of their process mature from tentative trial into definitive technique.

Each Source Book presents one project or group of related works that are significant to the practice and study of landscape architecture today. It is our hope that readers gain a sense of the project from start to finish, including crucial early concepts that persist into built form as well as the ideas and methods that are shed along the way. Design process, site dynamics, materials research, and team roles are explored in dialogue format and documented in photographs, drawings, diagrams, and models. Each Source Book is introduced with a project data and chronology section and concludes with an essay by an invited critic.

This series was conceived by Robert Livesey at the Austin E. Knowlton School of Architecture and parallels the Source Books in Architecture. Each monograph is a synthesis of a single Glimcher Distinguished Visiting Professorship. Structured as a series of discussion-based seminars to promote critical inquiry into contemporary designed landscapes, the Glimcher professorships give students direct, sustained access to leading voices in practice. Students who participate in the seminars play an instrumental role in contributing to discussions, transcribing recorded material, and editing content for the Source Books. The seminars and Source Books are made possible by a fund established by DeeDee and Herb Glimcher.

Foreword

Driving from Bellinzona to Locarno on the Via Cantonale in the Magadino plain, after having passed the church of the small village of Camorino and shortly after a railway underpass, the traveler's attention is drawn to a domed structure on the left-hand side. The self-supporting concrete dome is home to a garden center. Little does one realize when browsing through the plants, flowers, and pots that the office of one of Switzerland's best-known landscape architects is located on the garden center's grounds. The center was founded by Paolo Bürgi's late father, Carlo Bürgi. The roof's engineered aesthetic almost seems to anticipate the minimalist designs that result from the creative energy at work on this terrain in the southernmost part of Switzerland.

At the rear end of a rectangular piece of land used for the cultivation and propagation of the plants on sale at the center, Paolo Bürgi built his studio, where he has been practicing since 1977. At first glance, the studio is a conservatory that encloses a number of circular basins in which Mediterranean plants such as *Kentia*, *Strelitzia arborea*, *Cycas*, and *Papyrus* grow profusely. Hidden by plants and almost indiscernible to the visitor, a flight of stairs runs down to an office space below ground. There, a small team of landscape architects assists in turning Bürgi's ideas and sketches for villa gardens on alpine slopes and lakeshores, public plazas and parks, and master plans and city planning schemes into designs, renderings, models, and working drawings. Developed in his cavernous studio, Bürgi's projects literally see the light of day when they are brought up to the ground floor for further discussions with clients and collaborators, including artists and engineers, and when they are finally realized—in some cases by his own landscape construction firm. Like his design studio, the former is managed by Bürgi's wife Cristina, whose office space is located under palm trees, amidst the conservatory's plants. While maintaining its own microclimate through an automated system that opens and closes glass panels, the idiosyncratic studio–conservatory enables the people within to observe and participate in the changing of the seasons. Unobstructed views up the mountainside in the south, and across the plain toward the mountain ranges in the north, ground it in the Ticino landscape where mountains and water meet at the horizon.

In many of his landscapes Bürgi induces us to explore and imagine what lies beyond the horizon, as the title of this volume so aptly implies. Projects such as Cardada and the Terrace on the Forest, described in the following interviews, provoke or play on our feelings of awe, surprise, mystery, and sensation—feelings also commonly associated with the alpine landscape. Bürgi creates a unique tension in these and other designs that both enlightens and surprises, encourages and humbles us. It is one of his hopes that changing people's awareness and perception of the landscape will heighten their respect for and appreciation of the environment.

Bürgi's projects consist of grand or subtle gestures, accompanied by small, intricate design details that respond to the site's environmental conditions as well as to collective and individual users' needs and habits. Thus, on Kreuzlingen's Hafenplatz (Harbor Square) he chose to install custom-made concrete benches with a specific width—accommodating one person or a loving couple—colored in pastel shades that echo the natural light effects occurring on site. In a similar vein, he uses titanium—chosen for its warm reflection of light—for structural parts of the viewing platform on Cardada. With this use of color and light, Bürgi seems to hark back to the inspiration offered to him by Luis Barragán, whom he considers his teacher and primary influence. The Terrace on the Forest, finally, is bracketed by two wooden benches whose design accommodates a variety of body postures assumed when reading, conversing, and gazing out into the wilderness beyond.

Bürgi's gardens, parks, and landscapes seem to both suspend and be suspended in space and time. While he embraces the legacies of the modern architectural and artistic avant-garde in his work, his projects are also grounded in local traditions, cultures, and histories, and engage our senses. In this practice, which might be described in terms of the critical regionalism evoked by Kenneth Frampton in the 1980s, Bürgi captures the sensual qualities of a place and creates spaces that are meant to be moved through physically and/or mentally.

Movement plays a central role in Bürgi's work. He often prepares serial sketches that resemble film frames to visualize movement through his designed landscapes. In his 2002 project for the Von-Alten-Garten in Hanover, Germany, he used precisely this technique to explain what people would perceive when driving on the highway through what in the late-seventeenth century had been an elaborate baroque garden. His design proposal included the establishment of lines of trees that would form enclosures crossed by the highway and that would draw drivers' attention to past and present qualities of the landscape.

Research into the cultural, social, and natural history of the sites and their exploration as palimpsests is as fundamental to Bürgi's work as the use of centuries-old principles such as enforced perspective and the provocation of mystery, surprise, and caprice in his modern designs. Thus, different vegetative patterns in the Parco di Casvegno in Mendrisio, Switzerland, form follies situated along a path that resembles the beltwalks of eighteenth-century landscape gardens. Research for the above-mentioned project in Hanover unveiled an unknown axial relationship between the city's famous Herrenhäuser Gärten (Royal Gardens of Herrenhausen) and the destroyed Von-Alten-Garten. And by studying Kreuzlingen's old and recent history, Bürgi identified themes that ultimately formed the basis for the pictograms he had engraved into the cement slabs of the Hafenplatz.

When Bürgi, Giorgio Aeberli, his longstanding collaborator at the time, and I tested the scale and visual effect of the pictograms by laying their prints out along the pathways between planting boxes outside Bürgi's studio, the first snowflakes were falling. The close relationship between the inside and outside as manifest in Bürgi's studio–conservatory, and between design and production as exemplified by his design–build firm, influences the practice in his studio as well. Bürgi treats every project individually, regarding each task as an opportunity for himself and his small staff to learn and to experiment. Thus, on occasion I would be riding my bike to nearby businesses and industrial warehouses in search of suitable model-building materials. While the Ticino region provides a large part of the materials and inspiration for Bürgi's projects, the studio's immediate environs often become the testing grounds for one-to-one or scale models of design details. They also provide the setting for photos taken of models when the sun casts appropriate shadows before it disappears below the horizon.

Sonja Dümpelmann
University of Maryland

Data and Chronology

Cardada

CLIENT:
Cardada Impianti Turistici,
Switzerland

DATA:
371 acres (150 hectares; 1,500,000
square meters)

Material palette:
Geological observatory:
reinforced concrete, quartz resin
surface treatment, satin stainless
steel (handrails and symbols), rock
samples from the region, recycled
existing stones for the access path

Arrival plaza:
granite paving, wood and satin
stainless steel (bench, fountain),
grass

Viewing platform:
steel, titanium, local granite paving
stones, wood (forecourt bench)

New path:
tarring pavement with iron border
profiles

Game path:
marl path without border profiles,
wooden drainage channels

June–August 1995
A group of clients, including the
Swiss federal government and the
canton of Ticino, commissioned
the redesign of the cable car system
between Orselina and Cardada. Bürgi
begins to think about a possible
landscape intervention.

Fall 1995
Bürgi works on conceptual sketches
and forms a group of consultants,
including Guido Maspoli (biology);
Giovanni Bertea (history); Luca
Bonzanigo, Mario Codoni, Markus
Felber, and Paolo Oppizzi (geology);
and Flavio Paolucci (artist).

1996–98
Bürgi's office presents a formal
proposal to the clients, and the
design is approved.

1998–99
The first design scheme is developed,
and construction permits are
acquired.

1999
Construction begins, and work is
in progress throughout the year.
The arrival plaza, new path, game
path, landscape promontory, and
geological observatory are all
constructed contemporaneously
due to programming, transport of
materials, and organizational and
economic aspects.

Fall 2000
Construction is completed.

November 2003
The Cardada project is awarded
first prize at the Third European
Landscape Architecture Biennial in
Barcelona, Spain.

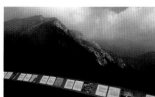

Kreuzlingen Hafenplatz

CLIENT:

City of Kreuzlingen, Bauverwaltung (Planning Department), Switzerland

DATA:

Park: 7.9 acres (3.2 hectares; 32,000 square meters)

Plaza: 1.73 acres (0.7 hectare; 7,000 square meters)

Material palette:

reinforced and refined concrete slabs (6.6 by 6.6 feet; 2 by 2 meters), gravel, wood benches, and painted concrete seats

Plants:

summer annuals: *Geranium*, *Begonia bulbosa*, *Canna indica* (only one species is planted each summer); winter annuals: *Viola* and *Tulipa*

January 2002

After being invited by the city of Kreuzlingen to participate in the competition for the redesign of its harbor square, Bürgi begins working on concept sketches and prepares a proposal.

February 2002

Bürgi's concept is chosen as the winning scheme, and the landscape architect begins to develop the design.

April 2002

Bürgi completes the master plan.

May 2002

Bürgi's office prepares construction documents.

June 2002

Bürgi's office builds a model of the proposal.

June 2002–April 2003

Detail studies of the paving, lighting, fountain, and benches are developed.

June–September 2002

Bürgi's office revises the construction documents.

September 2002

Permission documents for the beginning of construction are acquired.

November 2002

Construction work begins: the first stone is placed on site.

December 2002–April 2003

The old harbor walls and ramp are demolished; the concrete slabs of the square are put in place; the park areas adjacent to the square are modified according to the project; and lighting, flagpoles, benches, and the fountain are put in place.

May 2003

Kreuzlingen Hafenplatz opens with a celebration in which the mayor and citizens of Kreuzlingen participate.

December 2003

The project is awarded the "Bronze Hasenpreis Landschaft die Besten" 2003.

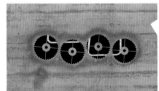

Terrace on the Forest

CLIENT:
Private (Swiss designer)

DATA:
Terrace: 151 square feet (14 square
meters)
Garden: 9,688 square feet (900
square meters)

Material palette:
wood (larch)

Plants:
endemic plants and trees, among
others: *Alnus glutinosa, Alnus
incana, Alnus rotundifolia, Populus
nigra, Salix alba, Salix rubra,
Fraxinus excelsior, Corylus avellana,
Phragmites communis, Carex sp.,
Typha sp., Juncus sp.*

December 1990
Bürgi receives the commission to
design a small garden with a terrace
in Ticino.

January–February 1991
Bürgi starts the first design sketches
and develops a proposal.

February–March 1991
The site is cleaned, unwanted plants
are removed, and scattered palms are
grouped together. General regrad-
ing and terracing is carried out, and
the foundations of the terrace are
constructed. The wooden structure
is assembled, and new specimens are
planted and grass is sown.

April–May 1991
Construction ends. Bürgi's office
develops a maintenance plan, and
the site is handed over to the client.

Conversations with Paolo Bürgi

Compiled and edited by Raffaella Fabiani Giannetto

Raffaella Fabiani Giannetto: **The well-known landscape historian and philosopher Massimo Venturi Ferriolo once said that it is unrealistic to attempt to define landscape. What is your position?**

Paolo Bürgi: I agree. You can't define landscape because it is a process; it is something in movement, and the result of the work of man. Think of agricultural or urban landscapes, for example: they are continually changing. The most important thing is to understand that landscape is a process. In addition to its material transformation, the perception of landscape is also subject to change depending on cultural memory and on the individual's own experiences. If you think of a place somewhere in the city—a plaza or a street— where you met your first boyfriend or girlfriend, that place will have a special significance for you. Every time you go there, you will see it with emotion because something happened there. Or

imagine a beautiful seashore somewhere in the Mediterranean region that was the site of an important battle in the past. Your knowledge of its history can change your perception and appreciation of that place. Of course, you cannot see what happened, because there's nothing left except the landscape, but as soon as you know that a battle took place there, the landscape becomes different in your mind. So this is also a change in a sense. Everything is conditioned by our imagination and knowledge.

RFG: **The simplicity and sobriety of your work seem to imply a minimalist leaning. How do you describe your design philosophy?**

PB: My work is not about trends; it is about the search for an essence and the possibility of evoking an emotion, a moment of serenity, so that as you leave a place you will look back at it, perhaps with some unanswered questions, and with a smile.

RFG: **How do you search for this essence?**

PB: Searching for the essential is a process that can take years of work. Take the Romanian sculptor Constantin Brâncuşi, for example. It took him more than twenty years to create what he thought was the essence of a child. His first sculpted head of a child is very naturalistic—you can see the hair, nose, lips, and many other details. Through the years Brâncuşi started to simplify the sculpture and take away those superfluous elements that do not constitute the intrinsic substance of his subject. In his later attempts, you can still recognize the forehead and the nose, but Brâncuşi kept reducing the work to its essence until, at the very last, the sculpture is a simple oval. You can still see the eyes in your mind—they are not there, but you see them. You see the nose, the mouth,

even the ears, although they are not sculpted. Of course, this creative process does not happen from one day to the next. So after many years you start seeing something that is not there, with your imagination.

RFG: **How can you achieve the same results in a design project?**

PB: In today's design, removing elements on a site is often as important as creating a dialogue between the new intervention and the site. Simplifying is necessary if you want to transmit something. I learned this lesson from the Mexican architect Luis Barragán. I met him several times; for me he was a maestro. He was able to place a wall in exactly the right place, with the right dimensions and the right colors. One of his last works, the private house he built in Mexico City for Pancho Gilardi, looks very simple from the outside: it is just a wall with a window and a

Luis Barragán, Pancho Gilardi's House, Mexico City, 1977

door. Inside, however, you enter into a beautiful atmosphere. It is essential to focus on what is important: the color blue, for example, on the back wall of the room with the swimming pool, emphasizes, and almost materializes, the midday light flooding the space from the skylight above, and the water of the pool carries the color inside the room, creating a beautiful contrast with the warm colors reflected from the other walls and the courtyard. Barragán managed to create a dialogue between the light shining in through the roof and the warm hues of the courtyard. It's a beautiful work.

Another example of a simple but eloquent intervention is the residential area Las Arboledas. Here Barragán placed a narrow pool of still water in the midst of a eucalyptus forest. You see the leaves of the trees reflected in the water and their shadows projected onto the white wall behind the trees and on the ground, together with the dappled light filtered through the branches; you can observe the movement of the leaves. Together with the real trees, these captured shadows and reflections create a beautiful dialogue between the few inserted elements and the existing ones. The atmosphere is very serene. If you can create a place conducive to silence and tranquility, these very qualities will allow you to focus on the few components that make up the design, like the volcanic formations that stand in contrast to the water and lawn surfaces in the Pedregal Gardens, also by Barragán.

RFG: **Barragán acknowledged surrealist painting—in particular the Greek-Italian painter Giorgio De Chirico's work—as having influenced his landscape projects. Do you draw inspiration from the visual arts? What enhances your creativity?**

PB: Painting is a great resource. I find surrealist artists, in particular, very intriguing, because they

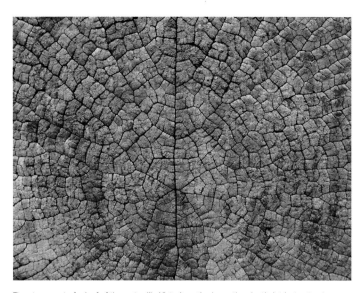

The stone cast of a leaf of the water lily *Victoria regia* shows the plant's intricate structure.

portray what they feel, rather than what they see, through metaphor and association. It's like visual poetry. My creativity is enhanced by anything that surrounds me. I am a curious observer; I am attracted by anything that stimulates my curiosity, be it a painting, a piece of music, or a particular plant. If you look at nature, you'll discover many inspiring details. Nature is amazing; everything has a reason and structure, and there is never too much.

I used to grow a water lily—a *Victoria regia*, a very beautiful tropical plant—in my office, which is located inside a greenhouse and features an indoor pond. I got a very young plant from a botanical garden and installed a solar panel to heat the water. The lily grew very fast, and in a few months its leaves started to emerge from the water, and I began to study them. The leaves have a rim, and when it rains, they look as if they are full of water but in reality they are not, because they have a system of microvalves that lets the

water seep through them. If you take the leaf and turn it upside down on the water, it sinks. Underneath the leaf is a structure that allows it to float when it is right side up. It's also equipped with thorns so that animals cannot eat it. One day I prepared a mold with a ring, took the leaf out of the water, turned it upside down, put the ring around it, and filled it with fluid concrete. A month later, I took this stone disk, washed it, and was left with an exact representation of the leaf structure. Looking at the disk, I realized that the plant's stem is not located at the center of the leaf, but in a position that corresponds to the golden section. From the stem, an amazingly proportionate structure branches out toward the edge of the leaf. This was an exciting discovery for me, because you can really see how nature works. Based on this observation you could design the structure for a roof, for example.

I believe that studying nature and works of art enhances your creativity and can provide you with answers. Mexican artist Chucho Reyes reinterprets the Mexican landscape in his paintings, in the colors of the pitahaya, a typical Mexican fruit. And the German artist Armin Sandig painted the sweet smell of eucalyptus. If you take a leaf from a eucalyptus tree and break it, the scent of it may very well compare with Sandig's visual interpretation.

In order to be creative, you need to have a flexible mind that is free from preconceived ideas, a mind that is ready to learn what you need in the different situations you face, and that allows you to modify your opinions whenever you need to. There is a beautiful documentary from the 1950s that shows Pablo Picasso at work. The first time I watched it, I noticed many affinities with the way we practice design. In one painting Picasso keeps changing the face of his subject, a woman. He paints so many layers—I counted at least thirty-eight—and each one is beautiful. This shows how the creative process can make you frantic and

restless, and that's exactly what happens when you work on details. It is said that the devil is in the details, because details take a lot of time, and you don't get paid for the work you put into them in the end. But details are very important; you have to keep working and working until you are satisfied. When you see this woman with her thirty-eight faces, you can feel how Picasso keeps searching for the exact expression he wants to give her.

RFG: **How did the idea to build an office in a greenhouse come about?**

PB: When I graduated from the University of Applied Sciences in Rapperswil, Switzerland, I first started working in a large room at my parents' place. It was also my bedroom. There I slept and worked and designed my first projects. Later on I was tempted to open an office in the city as the majority of my former classmates did. But my

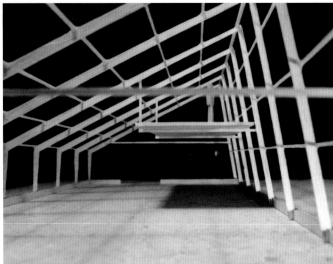

Top: Study model of Bürgi's office

Bottom: The transparent skin of Bürgi's office invites close interaction with the Ticino landscape.

Left: Bürgi's office under construction
Right: Plants filter the natural daylight and create
a pleasing work environment.

father convinced me to stay and build an office on the same land where he started his activity as master gardener in 1947. It was a large piece of land. I remember him taking twenty steps on a lawn and telling me, "This is our land. You can stay here and build your office. We can build a greenhouse—you know how beautiful it is to work in a greenhouse." My father was a charismatic and convincing person, so I decided to follow his advice. When I started sketching my studio, I was looking for a light structure with a transparent skin that would allow for maximum natural light. I also avoided subdividing the interior space with walls; instead, I inserted several ponds, where I grow exotic plants, either in water or soil. The glass and steel structure allows for a heightened perception of the passing of time, from sunrise to sunset, and from season to season. When the light is too strong, blinds can be lowered to protect from the sun. It is less tiring to work in an open space like this than

in a room surrounded by four walls where one is continuously exposed to artificial light. We use artificial light at night to light up the plants in the office. When everything else is dark, the transparent skin disappears, and the plants in the greenhouse merge with the outside landscape.

RFG: **Let's talk about your design process. When you work on a competition, for example, where do you start?**

PB: The first thing is a visit to the site. This is important. Let's take the competition we did for Töölönlahti Parks in Helsinki, Finland, together with a Japanese colleague. The brief called for the creation of a park near the heart of the city, where the main train station and other historical buildings are located. We went to the site and interviewed people to find out what they expected. We spent some time studying the place, walking, sitting, sketching, and taking pictures. Then we

Helsinki's vertical landmarks help visitors orient themselves.

researched the history of the site. Once you dive into the history of a place, the creative process has already started. We learned that the railway station was a point of exchange between Russia and Finland, St. Petersburg and Helsinki, so the movement of trains entering and leaving the city became a main focus point for us. We also noticed that while Helsinki is, and has always been, a flat city, its landscape is punctuated by many vertical elements—many of the city's churches have bell towers, but other buildings, such as museums and factories, the railway station, and the Olympic stadium, have towers as well. So the horizontal city is in sharp contrast with these vertical elements, which also appear on old drawings of the city. The urban fabric of Helsinki is very complicated: it is full of small islands—some with fields, some with buildings—like a maze of earth and water, of ports and fronts. But wherever you are in the city, if you see two towers, you know where you are—you are the third point

of a triangle. The towers allow you to orient yourself.

We also considered the different light conditions in summer and winter. In summer the sunrise is at around five in the morning and the sun sets around ten thirty at night, so people remain outside until very late. In the winter it's still dark at noon, before it gets a little bit lighter, but at three in the afternoon it's dark again. In these conditions, especially on foggy days, the city seems like a labyrinth, but as soon as you see the towers on the horizon, you can find your way. During the summer you also have to keep in mind that the city is made up of many islands, while in winter you can walk wherever you want, because the water is frozen and covered with snow.

Another important factor we took into account is scale. We noticed that Helsinki is made up of a variety of small places, which are beautiful and enchanting, such as small plazas, narrow

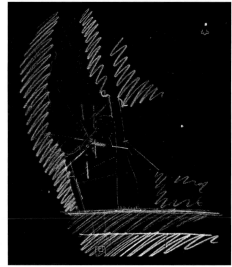

Left: Helsinki landmarks by night
Right: Preliminary sketch for the Töölönlahti Parks competition, describing, from top to bottom, the encounter with and the movement through the main elements of this landscape (hills, lakes, woods), the large meadow with the proposed trails, and a section of wooded park and the beginning of the city

streets, small fields, and small parks, but what the city lacks is an expansive space.

RFG: **So for you the site becomes the whole city; you don't limit your study to the boundaries of the intervention zone.**

PB: Yes, the site is the horizon. We don't just focus on the area where we intervene. In our proposal for the park we suggested a system of footpaths derived from a web of lines that connect Helsinki's vertical elements. When you walk along one of these paths, you always see one of the city's towers on the horizon. In the winter, when everything is frozen, you can walk over the lake in the direction of another tower. We proposed planting *Phragmites*, a water weed, to mark this web of lines leading across the lake and to protect the lake's shoreline. In the summer you can only look at the plants, but in the winter, when they are under the frozen surface, they mark the paths

that extend to the horizon, so you can actually walk along them. They play both an ecological and an aesthetic role.

Our reading of the landscape also allowed us to isolate some unique elements on the site, such as rock formations that seem to emerge smoothly from the ground and a birch wood with trees that stand very close to each other. We decided to focus on these landscape elements and proposed a succession of spaces that you experience when you approach the city by train: rock formations, a water surface, a wide field, and a small birch forest. The idea was to isolate and enhance these landscape elements so that they become easily readable. In fact, you can only distinguish them clearly during the summer months, because in winter the field and the lake become one large accessible surface.

For the rock landscape we proposed cleaning and polishing the stones we found on

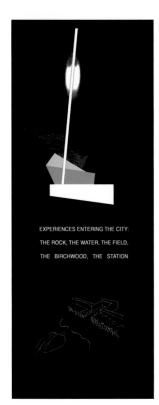

EXPERIENCES ENTERING THE CITY:
THE ROCK, THE WATER, THE FIELD,
THE BIRCHWOOD, THE STATION

TRAVERSING THE PARK:
THE BIRCHWOOD, THE WILDE FIELD,
THE LAKE, THE FOREST

THE PARTICULARITY:
IN THE RICHNESS OF SMALL SITES,
A WIDE OPEN SPACE

TRAVERSING THE EDGES OF TIME:
A PARK IN THE SUMMER,
A PARK IN THE WINTER.

site. They are like sculptures that remind you of the Finnish landscape. The train cuts through this rocky landscape, proceeds on a bridge over the water surface, and continues on to the field before entering the birch wood and finally the city. The birch wood is not just an informal forest; it becomes an architectural presence in the landscape. You pass through the trees before you enter the city of concrete, stone, and glass. You can imagine the magical atmosphere, especially in winter. We considered having this wood lit or keeping it dark so that you first experience the wide expanse of the field, then you go through a dark filter, and finally, you see the train station with its lights and colors. In the summer there is a Finnish festival during which lanterns are attached to birch trees for two days. So imagine entering the city by train during these days in August and going through a wood full of lanterns. I think it's important to understand the history of a place before you start a project. You need to

know these traditions; if you don't, the project can become very banal.

We also proposed to plant the field with seven wild flowers, to commemorate a beautiful Finnish legend that says that a girl who wants to get married has to put seven flowers under her pillow. We researched which flowers are the most typical in Finland, when they bloom, and their iconographic meaning. So the proposal for Töölönlahti Parks started with a study of an urban situation, the history of the city, and the importance of the horizon in Helsinki's urban fabric, and ended with these seven small flowers.

RFG: **Your design method implies an empirical approach: when you visit a site, you don't already know what you are going to do there. You don't carry a bag of tricks with you. However, your landscape projects all have an experiential-aesthetic dimension. What tools do you use to explore this quality?**

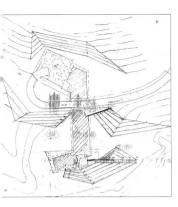

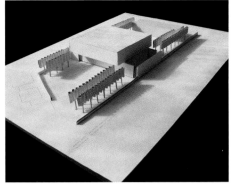

Sketching and model building are an important part of Bürgi's work.
Left: Sketch for a private garden in Connecticut
Middle: Model for the Memory Park in Milan, Italy
Right: Model for a private garden in Ticino, Switzerland
Opposite: Sketches and collages for the Töölönlahti Parks
competition, showing the procession of different landscape
elements as you walk or drive through the park

PB: Sketching is usually the first step. When I start sketching, I am completely free: I don't think about the project or the client, or about a form; I think about the place as if it were mine. The first sketches are very important, because they transmit not what you see, but what you feel. They are not perfect. They have mistakes, and they're not to scale. But they are very easy to read and very useful to explain your ideas and intentions. If I want to explore an idea, I start to sketch very fast; I don't waste time in details. I just start from the main lines, the main connections, the main idea. Then I put the first sketch aside and make a second one that is completely different, the opposite. I put it away and make a third one, a fourth one, a fifth one, until I can't anymore, until I run out of energy. Then the next day I look at the sketches again, and maybe I start to see something. I discuss the sketches with my colleagues, and we start to make some selections.

In addition to drawings we work a lot with models—mostly models that are done fast, just to find the proportions. We often test details at a one-to-one scale. For the landscape promontory at Cardada I made ten or twelve different small models to test the initial concept. Then we chose a few and made them bigger. For the handrail, for instance, we made many full-size models in wood and paper and spray-painted them in metal colors. We glued screws on them and added a net resembling the balustrade, so that in the end the models looked like the original.

For certain projects I like to draw a series of small sketches resembling frames of a film, to show how one moves through a space. I often accompany these sketches with writing—not just a few words to explain the images, but a continuous narrative that helps you read the images.

RFG: **A few critics today claim that traditional techniques of conceptualization and** representation are becoming increasingly inadequate and that designers need to put aside orthographic projections, such as the use of perspective so much associated with the picturesque, in favor of more temporal and synesthetic techniques, such as those used in choreography, which associates the sense of hearing with movement. What is your position?

PB: There are many different ways to explore your intention and to illustrate an idea. The Helsinki project, for example, could be explained with one of the first collages we made, which speaks about water, about grass, about woods. Then we made several more detailed sketches and collages that explore how you leave the city, how you walk through the woods and the field, and how you enter into the landscape of rocks. These sketches are not a representation of the real situation; rather, they are a representation of how you would feel when you go through the park in summertime or in winter. One of the sketches shows the city as a diffused landscape where you don't recognize what you see—what is water, what is an island, what is a tree or a building—and this is exactly the atmosphere of a city like Helsinki. In the end we used various types of graphic language in our proposal, including computer-generated presentation drawings.

RFG: **Your proposal for Helsinki was not completed—why?**

PB: It was an international competition with participants from all over the world, and we won third prize. The first and second prize–winning projects were more in tune with an artificial reconstruction of a Finnish landscape; they were very naturalistic. The critique of our project was very favorable, however. The jury thought that we gave an insightful interpretation of Finnish

Collage for the Töölönlahti
Parks competition

Drainage system at the Scuola Media di Cadenazzo in Ticino, Switzerland

history and culture. In fact, they were under the impression that a Finnish team designed our proposal and were quite surprised when they realized that it was a Swiss landscape architect with a Japanese collaborator. The competition had been organized by landscape architects who wanted to award a landscape firm with the first prize. I later learned from one of the jury members that they thought our proposal was very architectural and could not have been designed by a landscape architect. So we got the third prize.

RFG: **In Europe, particularly in Switzerland, the ecological aesthetic of the early seventies has done away with clearly recognizable manmade forms and has perpetuated the centuries-old imitation of nature, notwithstanding the presence of the Swiss landscape architect Ernst Cramer and his remarkable attempts to shake it off. Do you see design and ecology as mutually exclusive?**

PB: No, I don't. The protection of nature is important, of course, but human intervention doesn't need to be hidden, because it puts people in dialogue with the natural elements. An architectural landscape project is no less respectful of nature and ecosystems than a design that tries to hide the hand of man. As a student I rejected the gardening approach of some of my teachers. I did not understand it. I love plants—I worked as a gardener for two years, so I'm not afraid of getting my hands dirty—but I don't think one has to choose either the architectural approach or the naturalistic-ecological one. I think both can be integrated. For instance, my design for the Scuola Media di Cadenazzo, a junior high school in Ticino, was guided by both my architectural approach and my understanding of hydrological cycles. I designed a series of courtyards based on the amount of rainwater the area receives. I directed the water toward inlets and drains that are defined by simple linear forms and geometry.

Drainage system and fountain at the Scuola Media di Cadenazzo

As people move through these spaces, they become aware of the subtle balance between hydrology and gravity. I focused on the tactile quality of materials such as concrete, whose texture is enhanced by rainfall. So the design takes environmental processes into account, but its forms are not naturalistic.

RFG: **In one of your essays you claim that today we are witnessing a cultural and ethical impoverishment, mainly because human beings are getting increasingly disconnected from their environments. Do your design projects address these concerns, and if so, how?**

PB: I think the task of every landscape architect should be to address the well-being of human-kind through the shaping of our environment. Personally, I try to inspire people through my projects. I want them to gain a new sensibility, to appreciate the places they live in or visit. And I achieve that by exposing them to the processes of nature, to the inherent meaning of a place, which may emerge from its history, whether it be topographical, geological, or cultural. I believe that if we give people good reasons to respect their environment, the protection of nature will become a matter of fact instead of an extraordinary enterprise.

RFG: **Do your projects have a didactic scope?**

PB: My projects are not just about teaching. I strive for a more subtle approach—one that provokes people's imagination and elicits a personal response to a place. A few years ago I was invited to Hanover, Germany, to give a lecture, and I was asked to choose a place within the city that would be suitable for a landscape project. After visiting about a dozen potential places, I chose the site of the Von-Alten-Garten in the city's Linden district. Nothing remains of the old

This series of sketches for the Von-Alten-Garten project in Hanover, Germany, visualizes movement through the designed landscape.

baroque garden of Franz-Ernst von Platen, which was once located here; there is no trace of the original layout with its axes of symmetry and parterres. All we see today are a few old trees, the remains of a wall that used to surround the garden at a later stage, and a large, solitary terrace that was once attached to the palace, which was destroyed by bombing at the end of the Second World War. After the war the garden was damaged by urban redevelopment and the expansion of infrastructure.

I chose this site because it was very disturbed, yet it had a fascinating story. To me it was terrible to see the freeway traffic running through this historical park. I thought it was a crime. People would drive through the park, stop at a red traffic light, and drive on when the light turned green. They were completely unaware that under their feet was a place that was once so beautiful it attracted visitors from other countries. I never considered reconstructing

the original layout of the park or the original palace, because I think it is useless to give in to nostalgia and create historicist projects. Rather, I wanted to use the few existing fragments to transmit von Platen's original intention. His residence, once visually connected to the Duke of Hanover's palace, was a symbol of family prestige, and his park was open to the public. I worked with landscape elements such as rows of mature trees in order to reconstruct the atmosphere and the scale the park once had. Where the palace used to stand, I proposed a vertical garden made of a series of parallel metal walls that function as a supporting structure for climbers. Doors and windows pierce the structure and allow for glimpses of the interior corridors. I envisioned the climbers taking over this structure and forming a green palace that visitors can enter and discover. A structure like this tells a story to the people who visit this place; they are called to discover

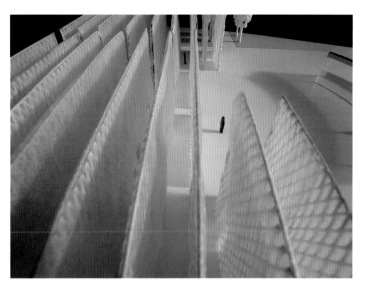

Model for the Von-Alten-Garten

it for themselves, with the eyes of their own imagination. If a project can achieve this, I believe it can also inspire a much-needed respect for the fragile and transient environment in which we live.

Cardada
Canton Ticino, Switzerland

At that precise moment
the man said:
What wouldn't I give for the bliss
of being by your side in Iceland
beneath a great motionless sky,
and to share this moment with you
the way I would music or the flavor of a fruit.
And at that precise moment
the man was with her, in Iceland.

—Jorge Luis Borges, "Nostalgia for the Present"

Cardada mountain overlooks Lake Maggiore in the foothills of the Alps in the Swiss canton of Ticino. In an effort to revive a long-lost respect for the environment in the area, Bürgi designed a number of discrete interventions on the mountain, which are united by their sensitive interaction with nature: a meeting place and arrival plaza where a cable car connects the town of Orselina to the mountain; a path suspended between the treetops and leading to a viewing platform; new connecting trails and a "game path"; and a geological observatory located on the summit, Cimetta. Each of these projects strives to stimulate the visitors' curiosity and enhance their perception of nature. In 2003 the Cardada project was awarded first prize at the Third European Landscape Architecture Biennial in Barcelona, Spain.

Raffaella Fabiani Giannetto: **How did the Cardada project begin? What were the circumstances that led to your involvement?**

Paolo Bürgi: In 1995 a group of clients, including the federal government of Switzerland and the canton of Ticino, commissioned the redesign of the cable car system that connects the town of Orselina to Cardada. The system was about thirty years old, so the township allocated some US$14 million for its modernization. Nothing else was supposed to change. But to me, the project presented an opportunity to rethink how people experience the mountain, which is a very important tourist site near Lake Maggiore and the city of Locarno. Some people believe that a project has to begin with a program, but this project began with a question: What do we want to find when we arrive at this mountain? For me, this simple question was enough to start researching the site. There was no program, nothing at all.

At the time the mountain looked like the periphery of the city. A cable car leads from Locarno to Orselina, where there is a hotel and a series of private houses. The place was very much disturbed by a number of small interventions, some of them designed to look natural, as well as by electrical lines and trails running adjacent to the houses. It resembled a suburban location where you don't feel immersed in nature. So the question was how to remedy this condition.

Our first proposal consisted only of text. We selected a few themes and created a sort of visual matrix that spelled out the relationships between the themes, the types of design interventions we envisioned, and their scope. The matrix illustrated the potential of the project to the clients, summarizing its main aspects:

Itinerary of discovery:
　—discovery of landscape
　—discovery of architecture
　—mystic and spiritual discovery
　—botanical discovery
　—geological discovery

Art of living and the quality of life:
　—gastronomy
　—leisure activities
　—play

Socio-cultural activities
　—classes
　—music
　—festivals

Each of these themes was discussed from different perspectives, such as ideas, themes, places, examples, potential developments, and research. We presented this matrix to the mayors of several towns, including Locarno, Brissago, Ascona, Muralto, Orselina, Brione, and Avegno, hoping that they would support my idea. They were all very interested in it from the beginning, but without a more detailed project proposal to look at, they could not understand how my ideas would be realized. Thus, after the initial approval,

I agreed to develop a full proposal, but I also asked to work with a group of consultants, including an artist, a biologist, a geologist, and a historian.

RFG: **What was the result of this collaboration?**

PB: As a first step we observed how people experience the landscape. In most cases tourists simply want to reach the highest point on the mountain. They take a chairlift from Orselina to Cimetta. Once they arrive, they enjoy the panorama and the fresh air, maybe sit down for a while, have a picnic and enjoy the view some more, before they go home—that's it. For me, this is a very reductive approach. A good example of this way of experiencing the mountainside are the belvederes we have in Switzerland, where aluminum plates contain etchings of the mountain range in front of you. Visitors stop at these places, read the names of Pizzo Vogorno or Monte Rosa, and then leave with a few names in their minds.

It's what I would call a landscape for consumption, similar to having a hamburger somewhere. I think that there must be something beyond the horizon, beyond what we actually see.

The question I posed myself was how to read the mountain, how to perceive it, in a different way. This part of Switzerland has a very diverse landscape that includes the Alps, the region of the foothills, and the Italian plain. This beautiful area speaks of a long cultural, geological, and botanical history. For instance, the birch wood at Cardada is a sign of emigration. Around 150 years ago this was a landscape of grassy fields used for grazing cattle and goats. The people living here were very poor, and many of them eventually emigrated to other countries, such as Argentina and the United States. The landscape was left abandoned, and many years later birch trees started to grow here spontaneously, because they were no longer grazed or cut down. The birch wood is thus a historical indicator. There are also

Top: Sketch of the arrival plaza in Cardada before the intervention

Bottom: Sketch of the surrounding landscape

other signs that tell a story, such as the lichens that grow on the rocks, which are proof that the air here is very clean, because lichens are sensitive to pollution. Or the presence of nesting eagles, which is an indication that this is not a noise-polluted environment. Moreover, from a geological point of view, the region is fascinating, because the Insubric line, the geological fault that separates the African plate from the European, runs through it. Ninety million years ago these plates moved fifty miles (eighty kilometers) horizontally and about ten miles (sixteen kilometers) vertically. At Cimetta you can actually see this division.

These observations helped me formulate my proposal, which emphasizes the landscape perceived through and beyond the horizon: that is, the immediate landscape of rocks, woods, lichens, and water as well as the landscape of geological time, ecological cycles, and human intervention. It's about the wind you perceive here and now, but also about the wind that erodes the land over centuries and millennia; it's about the dew you see and touch one particular morning, but also about the force of water over geological ages. I want to be sensitive to both the recent history and the past.

RFG: **You proposed a number of different projects on the mountain. How did you select the sites and how did you develop them?**

PB: I started with a few sketches of the area, and through these I selected several places that I found particularly interesting, places that have a fundamental presence on this mountain. In the end I proposed seven projects, five of which have been constructed. The first project is the arrival plaza in Cardada, outside the cable car station designed by Mario Botta. Originally there was only one path adjacent to the private houses. We proposed a new path that is far away from the buildings and leads to a viewing platform, the third project. Another trail connects to the chairlift

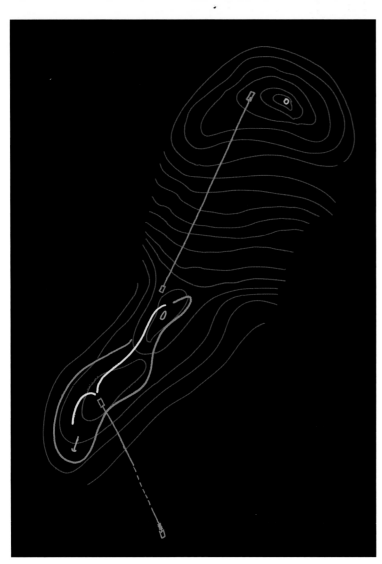

Top left: Sketch of the sites selected for possible interventions
Bottom left: The new trail connects several elements of the design (from bottom to top): the viewing platform; the arrival plaza of the cable car station; a small church plaza designed for an existing church; and the departing point of the chairlift leading to Cimetta
Top right, bottom right: Besides the five main interventions at Cardida, Bürgi also designed a small church plaza for an existing church, recycling stones from the old cable car station.

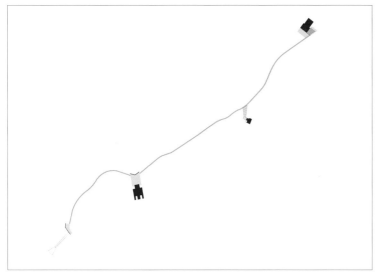

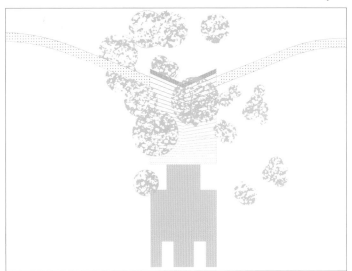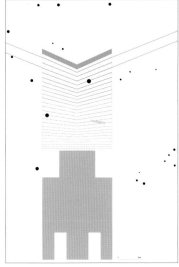

Plans of the arrival plaza

and to the fourth project, the game path around the hill. The fifth intervention, the geological observatory, is at Cimetta.

The arrival plaza is an important place. It's where the excursion begins and ends; it's a meeting place. The pavement consists of granite blocks separated by grass strips. I wanted a pattern that symbolized the transition from the city to the landscape. The strips of granite located closer to the cable car station are very narrow, but they get larger as you move away. The choice of the pattern was also motivated by costs. By alternating standard slabs of granite with slabs specifically cut for this project, we significantly decreased the cost of construction. The layout of the pavement also suggests the two possible directions of movement, left or right, which are also emphasized by the form of the bench that borders the plaza and bounds the space. The dimensions of the bench allow you to lie down, sit, or use it as a table if you just want to eat something.

RFG: **The plaza also has a fountain, and fountains are an important element in your work. Can you explain what is different about this one?**

PB: In a place like this a fountain is necessary not only because it is a lively element, but also because it provides potable water. Unlike my other fountains, which I built in concrete, this one is made from a single piece of hundred-year-old oak. I worked closely with carpenters to give form to this large trunk. I wanted just one jet of water falling onto the wood and flowing down until it is collected by a stone element with a central hole. We made many sketches and models as work progressed. I chose oak because it is a very durable wood, but also because constant contact with water changes its appearance. After a while a patina began to form on the wood, and a few months later it became almost black because of the tannin it contains. I also wanted the fountain to be

The strips of granite and grass get wider toward the end of the plaza, signifying the change from the city to nature.

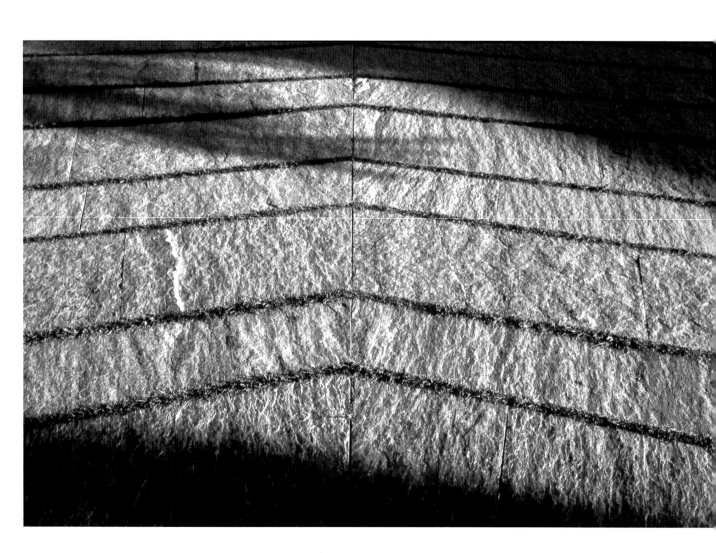

Top Left: Arrival plaza under construction

Top Right: Choosing the tree trunk for the fountain

Bottom Left: Bürgi worked closely together with carpenters to fashion the trunk into a fountain.

Bottom Right: Positioning of the fountain on the plaza

amusing. Children can play with the water, or they can place stones on the fountain in order to try to stop the flow. Dogs can drink the water jetting out from the lower part.

The fountain is detached from the ground to prevent water on the ground from rotting the wood. It is large and heavy, so it cannot be moved and is resistant to vandalism.

RFG: **Describe the viewing platform.**

PB: The idea for this project came from my opposition to the traditional way of approaching the landscape. Instead of cutting down trees in order to clear the view to a beautiful panorama, I imagined flying through the treetops to the point where the landscape below is revealed. I thought this would be a far richer experience. Imagine moving between tree trunks, branches, and lichens and suddenly coming to a place where beautiful views of the landscape open up before you. In my very first sketches I tried to capture this experience, but I had only vague ideas of how the platform might look; I drew something that involved entering through the trees and disappearing behind them.

Before we started working on the design of the structure, we surveyed the entire hill, calculating the trees' heights. Then we drew a path that attempts to create a dialogue with the existing vegetation, with the aim of making the elevated walkway to the viewing platform feel as if it had been there forever. We made more than twenty models. I knew that I wanted a light structure, with columns leaning outward to suggest movement. In order to find the right distance between the two supporting columns, I traced a 144-foot-long (44 meters) path on the ground in my mother's orchard. The distance between two existing cherry trees felt like the right distance between the columns.

A granite grill collects the water at
the base of the fountain.

Top: The viewing platform among the tree tops

Bottom and opposite: The approach to the viewing platform is
an experience in itself.

Top: View of Lake Maggiore from the viewing platform

Bottom: Model of viewing platform

The two materials of the load-bearing structure—
titanium and steel—create an interesting contrast.
The titanium warmly reflects the light at night.

Next we chose the materials. The load-bearing structure is made of steel and titanium. Titanium is a wonderful material, because it reflects the colors of its surroundings, so it feels very warm. Steel, on the contrary, looks and feels like ice. Together they create a beautiful contrast. The railing is made with a thin-gauge steel net and built higher than required by law, because I wanted people to feel safe. The holes in the net are small enough to not allow children to insert their feet in it or climb it.

I also wanted visitors to be able to see the landscape at night, because the experience is very different than during the day, when you can see the mountain, the larch wood with its dark green, dark blue, brown, and gray colors, and the lake, which changes from a deep blue to silver if there are passing clouds. At night you are in a very different place. You see the lights from the surrounding cities, which appear closer than they do during the day; you can see where people work,

where they live, and how they move. In order to make the platform accessible at night, I inserted a number of small light-emitting diodes into the granite pavement. These lights work with a solar panel positioned on top of the structure, and they lead you to the outer terrace when it's dark. In winter you see these blue lights shining through the snow. It is wonderful to see how the landscape changes throughout the year and from day to night.

RFG: **The granite pavement has symbols carved into it that refer to ecology and the elemental structures of living organisms. Does the platform have a meaning that goes beyond its immediate scope as a viewing point?**

PB: Yes. The experience of walking through the trees, and of seeing and touching the lichens, as well as my thoughts about biological time, urged me to embed in the path a sort of narrative that is

Viewing platform under construction

Viewing platform at dusk

Top: At night a series of small lights leads out to the viewing platform.

Bottom: The approach to the viewing platform in winter

The symbols carved on the pavement of the viewing platform include references to living organisms, such as signs for specific animals and plants, as well as the shape of DNA or the structure of a single cell.

made up of symbols. The purpose of the carvings is not to teach but to intrigue, to add a sense of mystery. They are not accompanied by any explanation. The symbols range from the shape of DNA to that of a single cell, from the structure of tissue to the outline of whole individuals. A maple leaf and a buzzard's footprint stand for individual organisms, while the engraving of the Fibonacci sequence suggests an ecosystem. The first two numbers in a Fibonacci sequence are zero and one, and each subsequent number is equal to the sum of the previous two, so all numbers are connected, just like everything is connected in an ecosystem. Ecosystems are so delicate and fragile that every human intervention has consequences in the "sequence."

But this is not the only story that this project tells. I believe that knowing something about the history of a landscape and its inhabitants can change your perception of it and transform it into a very different place. Once

you reach the edge of the viewing platform, you are suspended over the open landscape. You have left the trees behind and are confronted with a vast space, with Lake Maggiore below and the mountains on the horizon. This is not merely a beautiful view, though. The lake, for example, is not just a place where people go water skiing, windsurfing, or scuba-diving; it once was an important transportation route used by the Romans to move stone for their building projects, in particular a very beautiful pink stone from Angera. In the distance you see the Brissago Islands, which are famous today for their botanical gardens, though many years ago they were completely wild. A Russian baroness who was a student, and apparently also the lover, of the Hungarian pianist Franz Liszt constructed the gardens. But there are many other people connected to these islands, such as the German writer Stefan George and Claus Schenk Graf von Stauffenberg, the German officer who made an

Left: Aerial view of the platform,
with Lake Maggiore and the Brissago Islands below
Right: The handrail is inscribed with symbols and names of
people and locations connected to the area.
Opposite: The carving of the Fibonacci sequence hints
at the delicate balance of interconnections found in ecosystems.

attempt on Adolf Hitler's life. At some point in their lives these people came here, and that is why I had their names inscribed on the handrail of the viewing platform.

Another symbol on the railing speaks of a past tradition: the image of a rare fern called *Adiantum capillus-veneris*, whose rhizomes were used more than a hundred years ago to make a restorative drink called capilèr. The drink was very famous among the English tourists who used to come to Lake Maggiore during their summer vacation. Of course, visitors today may not be familiar with this plant and its past uses, or with the history of the place, but when they see the signs and the names of people or locations inscribed on the handrail, I hope they will wonder about the relationship of these words and symbols with the lake. I deliberately provide no answers. I hope that people will want to find out on their own and perhaps come back one day. A poem by Jorge Luis Borges called "Nostalgia for the Present"

is also inscribed on the handrail. It aptly captures the spirit of this project: it is about the idea of being present somewhere with your imagination alone; it speaks of the appreciation of the present, of what you see, and of the awareness of passing time, of what is no longer visible and belongs to history.

RFG: **What happens once you leave the viewing platform?**

PB: You can trace your steps back toward the arrival plaza and then follow the other trail that leads to the chairlift. Along this trail a sign directs visitors to my fourth project, the game path.

RFG: **Why did you give it that name?**

PB: As you walk along the game path, you discover a number of games, placed about three hundred feet (one hundred meters) apart from each other,

Left: On the merry-go-round along the game path visitors can experience centrifugal force.

Right: The sound seesaw emits sounds as you step and balance on it.

that let you explore the laws of physics. I wanted to create a path that leads through the beauty of the forest, but at the same time provides people with ways to amuse themselves. The first game is a small merry-go-round for one person that lets you experience centrifugal force when you step on it and start spinning. As you raise or lower your arms, your speed changes. Another game is the sound seesaw, which plays sounds as you try to balance on it. And then there are the parabolic mirrors, which can be used to communicate at a distance. These games are meant to delight people as they walk along the path. You also have the option of just sitting down and resting on benches along the way. It's a very comfortable path to walk on, as it never slopes very sharply, so it should be possible for people of all ages to walk on it in a relaxed manner, side by side.

RFG: **How did you decide on the position of the path and its route?**

PB: The path traverses a very interesting landscape that includes four zones, each of which has a different dominant tree. For example, the section that is north-exposed, which is cold and humid, close to the cable car station, is dominated by silver fir trees (*Abies alba*). There is nearly no sun here. The atmosphere is very special because the trunks of these trees are very dark and the leaves are dark green. This is the coolest place in the summer, while in winter it's very cold. The part of the path that crosses this landscape is entirely new.

The next section, to the northeast, is where beech trees (*Fagus sylvatica*) grow. Here the atmosphere is completely different. The trunks are gray and look almost as if they were made of concrete, while the leaves are light green. On the west side the dominant tree is the larch (*Larix europea*). Here the colors change again; sunlight penetrates and the ground is brighter. Ferns also grow here, and it is much warmer. The last section of the path is a wood planted with Norway spruce

Left: The parabolic mirrors can be used to communicate at a distance.
Right: A beech tree (left) among silver fir trees along the game path

Left: Beech and silver fir trees along the game path
Middle: Benches along the game path provide a place to rest.
Right: A larch tree (right) and silver fir trees along the game path

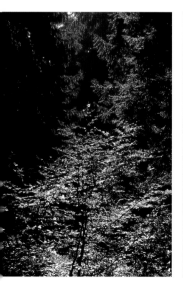

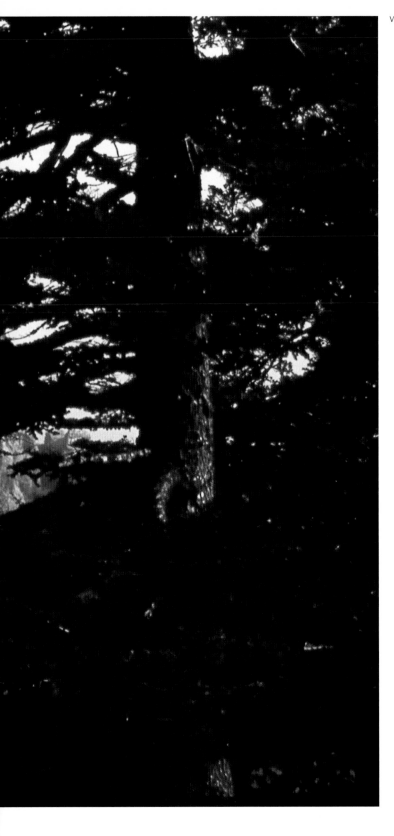

Vegetation along the game path

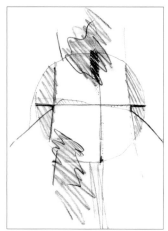

Left: Site of the observatory at time of construction
Right: Early sketch of the observatory

(*Picea abies*) some decades ago. The trees are planted in an orderly fashion, and their trunks are very straight. Hazelnut trees (*Corylus avellana*) dominate the southernmost part of the path; here it is very mild even in February because of warm air coming from the lake, while in summer it gets very hot. Even though the entire path is less than a mile long, it gives visitors the unique opportunity to observe these dominant trees in their diverse environments.

RFG: **Describe your last intervention at Cimetta.**

PB: When you take the chairlift to the top of the mountain, which is 5,500 feet (1,670 meters) above sea level, you come to the geological observatory. Originally the summit was crowded by various structures and wasn't very inviting. I proposed to build a circular platform that you gradually discover as you walk along a path. As you approach it, you only see its edge and part of the handrail. I wanted the project to refer to the presence of the Insubric line and to the tectonic movement of the European and African plates.

As a first step we surveyed the hill with its stone outcroppings and selected samples of stone from the two plates. We aligned the stone samples on a concrete disk marked by a red line symbolizing the separation between the plates. The metamorphic stones from the European plate are grayish in color, and I placed them closer to the symbolic Insubric line, because they are younger, while the ocher stones from the African plate, which are two hundred to three hundred million years old, are farther away from it. The handrail of the observatory contains information about the stones.
I also wanted to represent geological time. Again we engraved symbols in the pavement, such as trilobites, a fern, a dinosaur, and many others, through geological time up to human beings.

Left: Path to the observatory
Middle: Sketch of the observatory at night
Right: Observatory under construction;
Paolo Bürgi with the group of geologists.
Bottom: Rock outcroppings on the summit

View of geological observatory from above, showing
the marble slab leading up to the platform

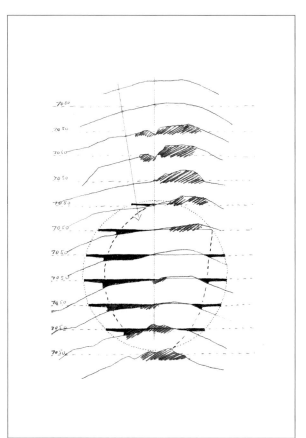

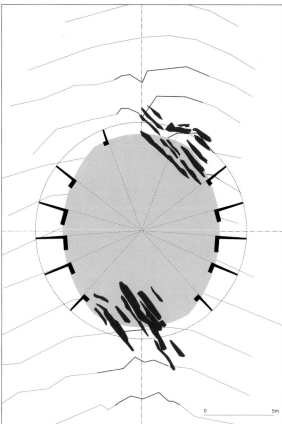

Left: Study in section of the relationship between the actual topography of the site and the proposed intervention
Right: Plan of the observatory with superimposed sections

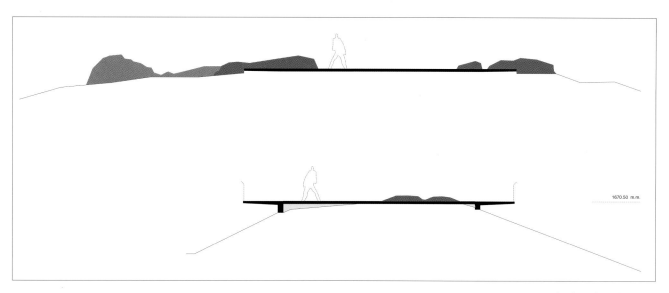

Sections of the observatory

through geological time up to human beings. The positioning of these symbols on the disk in relation to the stones and to each other allows you to understand the stones' age. Some of the stones are already showing signs of wear, but this is a reminder of geology, of the effects of erosion and time. That's also why I chose marble for the last part of the path leading to the disk. Marble is not as hard as granite or the surface of the disk, which is made of concrete covered with quartz sand, so in a few decades the marble steps will also be showing signs of erosion. It was difficult to explain to the committee that it is worth it to wait fifty years before the stone is the way I want it.

RFG: **In *The Afterlife of Gardens*, John Dixon Hunt says that "a garden without an afterlife is worth little." What are your thoughts?**

PB: I agree. I often go back to visit my projects once they have been completed. For me it is an excellent way to test the success of my designs. I like to observe people's reactions and see what surprises them. Once I accompanied a classical choir to Cardada. When we reached the viewing platform, they were so enthusiastic they started to sing. It was an incredibly gratifying experience.

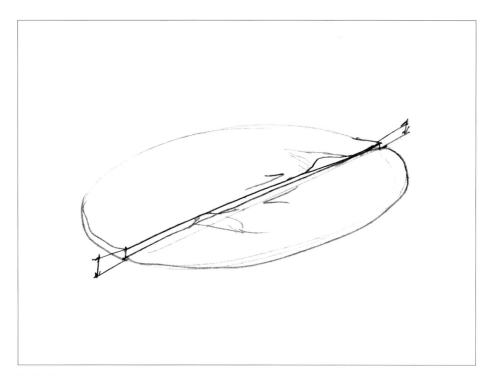

Top: Sketch of the Insubric line

Bottom: Plan of the Insubric line

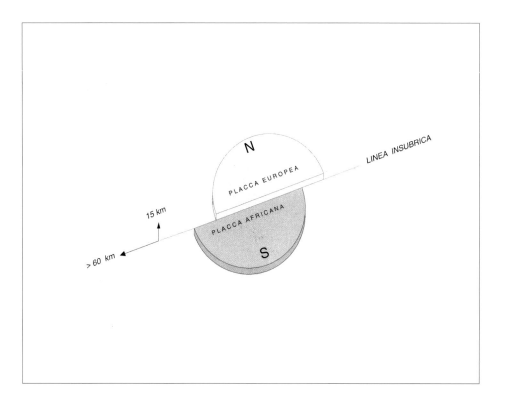

Top: Rock samples from the two plates are displayed on the concrete disk.
Bottom: The plan of the geological observatory shows the red line symbolizing the Insubric line and the placement of the rock samples in relation to it.

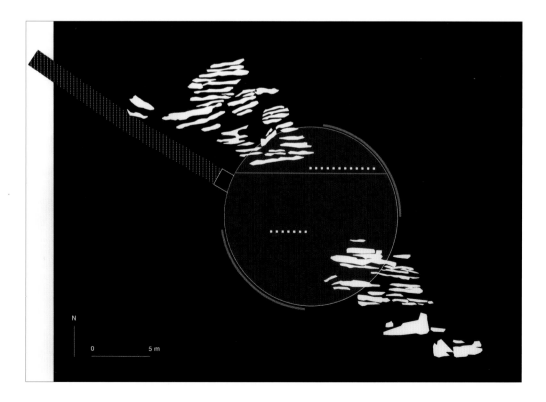

The handrail contains information about the movement of the tectonic plates and the rock samples displayed on the observatory. Symbols engraved in the observatory disk represent geological time.

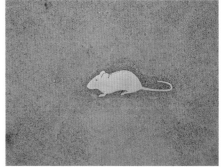

Left: Detail of geological observatory with symbol of snail

Right: Engravings of fern and mouse symbols

Kreuzlingen Hafenplatz

Canton Thurgau, Switzerland

Kreuzlingen, like many other cities along the coast of Lake Constance, which separates Switzerland from Austria and Germany, tended to ignore the lake for many years, until 2002, when the city initiated a competition for the redesign of its Hafenplatz (Harbor Square). Paolo Bürgi's winning scheme was completed in 2003 and was awarded the "Bronze Hasenpreis Landschaft die Besten."

Raffaella Fabiani Giannetto: **What did the site look like before you started your project?**

Paolo Bürgi: The configuration of the site did not allow for direct access to the water. The reed-lined coastal areas mediating between land and water were far from elegant, and there was a round wall that obstructed the view of the city from the water and vice versa. The place was crowded with a confusion of parking lots, trees, flowerbeds, and street furniture. People had no real plaza or space in which to meet. Moreover, the presence of the nearby historical Seeburg Park was not acknowledged in any way, because the existing planting obscured the entrance to the park.

RFG: **What was your first reaction to the site?**

PB: I thought creating a visual connection between the city and the lake was absolutely essential, because Kreuzlingen is a big tourist destination, so the approach to the city from across the lake needed to be taken into consideration. I also wanted to give people as many opportunities as possible of being in touch with or close to the water, and I thought it was equally important to connect the lake to the park in a more transparent way.

RFG: **How did you implement your ideas?**

PB: First we started to simplify the plaza by taking away anything that was superfluous, such as the small shrubs hiding the entrance to the park. I also

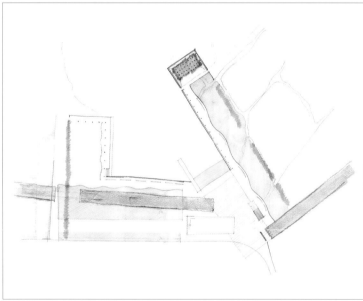
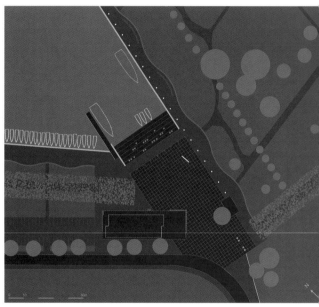

Top left: The site before the intervention

Top Right: View of Lake Constance

Bottom Left: The Kreuzlingen master plan shows the new connection
Bürgi created between land and water and the simplification of the site.

Bottom Right: Plan of the Hafenplatz

Left: The model shows the graduated ramp leading to the water.
Right: The flagpoles contrast with the wide horizontal square.

removed the round wall that prevented access to the lake and instead proposed a large plane that meets the water with gently graduated terracing. Then I contrasted this wide horizontal space with a series of vertical elements: a row of flagpoles on the side of the square parallel to the water. The flagpoles can also be used to announce cultural events taking place in the city, such as concerts, exhibitions, and so on. In addition to the flags, I wanted to insert another element that would make the dimensions of this plaza more legible, so I added a long flowerbed that borders the marina.

RFG: **Why is the flowerbed planted with a single plant species?**

PB: I wanted it to be planted with thousands of red geraniums because the flowerbed had to be a visually strong architectural feature that connects the lake to the city. Too many plants or too many colors would have failed to make the

connection visible. This is something I learned from the Swiss landscape architect Ernst Cramer. He once said something that I'll never forget. I was still in school at the time and went with Cramer and other students to visit a new housing development, which consisted of a series of scattered houses. The landscape architect, who was more of a gardener than an architect, had planted a number of different shrubs and trees, and inserted paths and benches. It was a very disorderly site. One student asked Cramer what he would do to remedy the situation, and he replied with one simple phrase, "a hundred *Platanus*" (plane trees). In an atmosphere that is disturbed by a myriad small interventions, you must choose a strong architecture that functions as the connective fabric. The same was true at Kreuzlingen: there were too many distractions, and nothing that caught the eye.

One of two existing elements that I left on site is a tree, a Weeping Golden Ash (*Fraxinus*

Top: A linear flowerbed borders the marina.

Bottom: At night the small lights inserted in the concrete paving and the lit fountain create a magical atmosphere.

The gate of the historic park stands in axial connection to Kreuzlingen's old castle.

excelsior 'Pendula'). Some people wanted to remove it, but I insisted on keeping it, because in the composition of the plaza it was the only tree, so it functioned like a monument. At the same time it creates an atmosphere: one can imagine placing a few chairs and a table under the tree during the summer. The other existing element that I left is a gate that leads to the old castle located in the park. I cleared the space around the gate, so that its axial connection to the historic building would be revealed again, the only difference being that now you can walk around the gate, rather than simply through it, as would have been the case in the sixteenth century.

I believe that in order to transmit ideas, in order to communicate with the users of a site, you must choose a few important elements and make people feel their presence. So, for instance, there are no other strong colors on the plaza and no other large plantings that might compete with the vibrant red geraniums of the flowerbed. Of course,

the situation changes at night, when you can't see the colors of the water, grass, or flowers. That's why I inserted seventy-four diodes in the pavement. These small blue lights are intended to catch the attention of passersby at dusk and draw them into the plaza. They also create a beautiful atmosphere early in the morning, when it's misty.

RFG: What about the seating you designed for the plaza?

PB: At the beginning I didn't think about including any street furniture, but the clients wanted people to be able to sit near the water, so I decided to add concrete benches. I made many models of these seats, because I had to find a good way to arrange them on the ramps by the water. They also needed to be resistant to vandalism—if they were made out of plastic, for example, you would soon find them floating in the water. They also needed to be heavy, so that kids could not

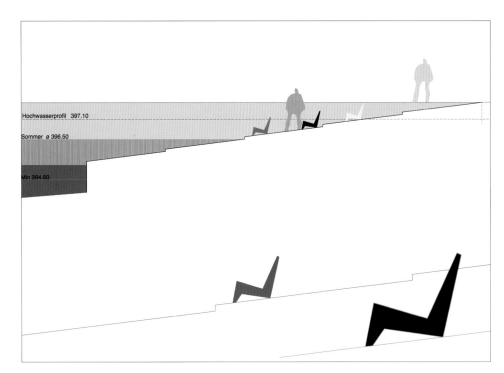

Hochwasserprofil 397.10

Sommer ø 396.50

Min 394.60

Top: Section of the concrete seats

Bottom: Detail

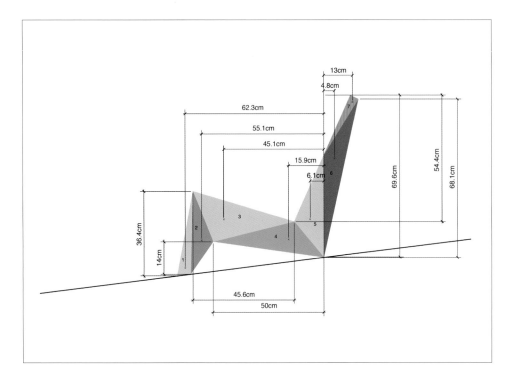

Left: View of the lake from the square, with the concrete seats on the ramp
Right: The light pastel colors of the concrete seats reflect the natural colors of the water and sky.

turn them around or upside down. And of course, the most important requirement was that they be comfortable. The material I chose is concrete formed with a mold that makes it very smooth. We painted the concrete with a special opaque paint to give it very light pastel colors that blend with the atmosphere.

RFG: **You also designed long wooden benches on the edges of the lake. Why did you decide to have two different types of seats? Doesn't this contradict your quest for the essential and the simple?**

PB: I don't think so. The wooden benches, with their high backs, have a serpentine form that echoes the waves of the geraniums. Together they draw visitors inward from the lake to the park. So even if the benches are meant for rest, they suggest movement. The concrete seats have a different, calmer purpose. You can sit on them

and contemplate the horizon; parents can sit here and watch their children play with model boats on the water. The dimensions of the concrete seats are carefully chosen: they are thirty-three inches (eighty-five centimeters) wide, which makes them very comfortable to sit on alone, but they are also big enough for lovers who want to sit close to each other.

RFG: **Describe the fountain, another important architectural element of your design.**

PB: The form of the fountain derives from my experiments with how water flows and falls. It's a continuous theme in my work. This fountain, in particular, speaks about erosion. It is meant to suggest how water can wear through stone with the passage of time. It is made of concrete so smooth that it feels like glass. I also wanted the fountain to be visible at night, because this place is very lively, especially during summer nights.

The fluid shape of the wooden benches evokes the movement of water.

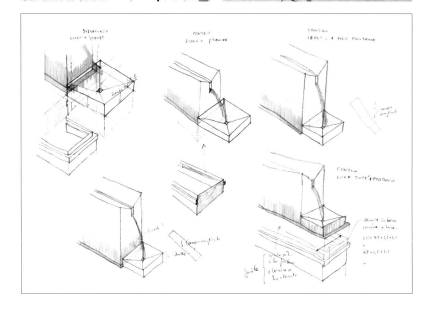

Top: The fountain is made of smooth concrete.

Middle and bottom: Sketches of the fountain

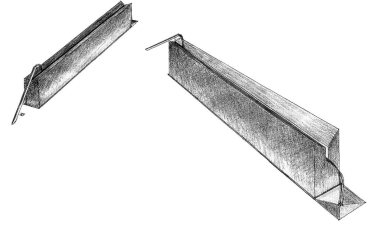

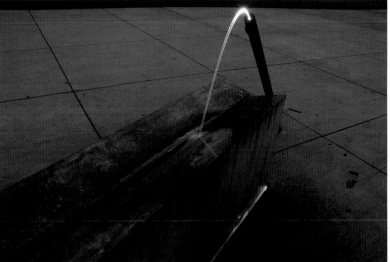

White lights are hidden at its base and inside the pipe supplying water, so as the water pours from the pipe, light streams with it. While during the day the fountain appears as one heavy piece of concrete, at night it seems to float weightlessly above the plaza.

When I designed the square, I was interested in the relationship between the fountain and the ground, and the horizontal surfaces of the plaza and the sky. At night the blue lights embedded in the concrete paving are meant to echo the starry sky. The flagpoles are also lit at night to highlight their function as marker and gateway alike, both to the lake and to the town.

RFG: **The large, brushed flagstones of the plaza have symbols inscribed in them. What is their meaning?**

PB: The symbols are meant to draw attention, especially tourists' attention, to aspects of Kreuzlingen's history as well as to its contemporary activities in areas such as education, culture, the environment, and industry. For example, one of the emblems represents the cocoa seed because chocolate is produced in the area, while another depicts a Scottish Highland steer, an endangered breed of cattle that was famously cared for and bred by Guido Leutenegger, one of Kreuzlingen's Green Party councilors.

These symbols are set quite far apart from each other, and each one of them is repeated twice on the square. In order to find an exact position for them, we made printouts, laid them one by one on the plaza, and walked through them to test their sizes and set the distance between them. Then we used sandblasting to engrave the concrete.

RFG: **Since its completion your design has won both praise and criticism, the latter particularly**

KREUZLINGEN HAFENPLATZ

At dusk the fountain is lit below and seems suspended in air.

A set of symbols inscribed in the pavement reflects aspects
of Kreuzlingen's history and culture:

Left column, top to bottom:

Aluminum and synthetic layers
rollware industry

The cross refers to the origin of
the town's name (*Kreuz* means
"cross" in German).

Fashion industry

Settlement of Highland cattle in
protected areas

The peacock goat is an
endangered species
reintroduced in the Kreuzlingen
Seeburg Park.

Professional photo processing
industry

Middle column, top to bottom:

Cross-country motor vehicle
industry

Helen Dahm, born in
Kreuzlingen, was the first
woman awarded with the
Zürcher Kunstpreis (Zurich art
award).

The Aesculapian staff refers to
the dynasty of a well-known
doctor.

Project to resettle a white stork
colony in Kreuzlingen

The *Appenzeller Spitzhauben-
huhn* hen is an endangered
species that was reintroduced
in the Kreuzlingen Seeburg
Park.

The cocoa bean refers to the
production of chocolate in
the area.

Right column, top to bottom:

Metal manufacturing industry

The spade refers to the town's
education system, the so-
called *Spatenkultur* (spade
culture), introduced in 1833,
in which teachers had to learn
elementary agriculture skills in
addition to the study of other
subjects.

The owl stands for wisdom.

Wooly pig settlement in
protected areas

Plastic bottle safety closure
system industry

Ballpoint pens and writing
components industry

The symbols are sandblasted into the concrete.

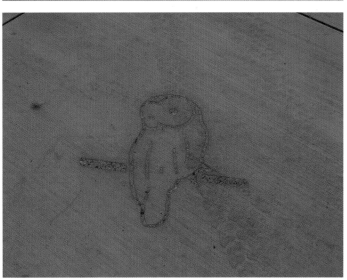

Sandblasting of the symbols

for the amount of concrete used. Do you think the project is successful from environmental and sociocultural points of view?

PB: One can criticize the use of concrete because it's a nonpermeable surface, and some people regard it as inhospitable, but at Kreuzlingen I don't think this is an issue. Certainly two miles (three kilometers) of harbor can endure a few thousand square feet of cement paving, from which rainwater can run off directly back into the lake.

I think that the project is successful, because the square has become the place in Kreuzlingen where people meet. At lunchtime students go there and have a bite before they return to school. People skate on the plaza in the area behind the flagpoles, and children use it in a multitude of ways. And during the summer it is incredibly lively, because it hosts numerous festivals.

The plaza has become a central meeting place.

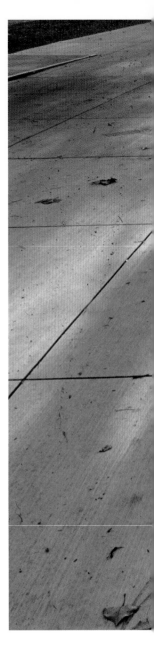

Terrace on the Forest

Sementina, Canton Ticino, Switzerland

"**Born to see, trained to perceive.**"

—Johann Wolfgang von Goethe

In 1991 a Swiss designer commissioned Paolo Bürgi to design a private garden. The project consists of a small terrace overlooking an untouched section of alluvial landscape. By means of its small scale and the materials used, Bürgi's design emphasizes the secular sacredness of the place, which emerges from the contrast between wilderness and culture.

Raffaella Fabiani Giannetto: **In your writings you often emphasize the need to see beyond the physical boundaries of a place and to discover the horizon. At Cardada this implies the humbling experience of comparing our limited time in this world with the millions of years of geological time, while at Kreuzlingen our experience is enriched by the opportunity to contemplate the calm surface of the lake, which reflects a vibrant urban life. Did your perception of the horizon also influence your project for a private garden in Sementina, the Terrace on the Forest?**

Paolo Bürgi: Yes, taking the horizon into account is an important part of my design philosophy. When I designed this small garden, I was fascinated by the site, an alluvial landscape that people have avoided since the last century—once because of malaria and now because it's visually unattractive. It looks like a jungle. I believe that most people would be inclined to block the view to this forest, because they would regard it as disorderly and abandoned, but to me it's important to see beyond the physical appearance of a landscape. The forest is a rare example of untouched nature, and untouched nature is something sacred.

Take, for instance, the famous Galapagos Islands, where in some parts you must walk along designated paths, from which you are not permitted to stray. When you want to leave, you have to retrace your steps. This means that there may be untouched ground only a few feet from the path. To me this is an incredibly strong notion.

View of the alluvial forest landscape from the terrace

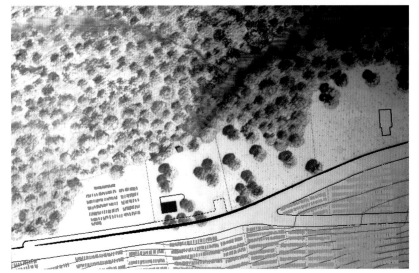

Left: Site plan showing the terrace in red
Right: The terrace is suspended over the wild landscape
bordering the garden.

Everything there is natural in the true sense of the term, just as it is in the forest near the site at Sementina, which has a thriving and very diverse ecosystem.

RFG: **Isn't beauty an indispensable quality for visual and spiritual gratification? In his acceptance speech for the Pritzker Architecture Prize, Luis Barragán suggested that the word "beauty" is in danger of disappearing from the vocabulary of architects and critics. What are your thoughts?**

PB: I think what is changing today is the definition of beauty. We are no longer speaking of beauty in the classical sense, because we are rediscovering a taste for the romantic and the sublime. This wild forest with dense vegetation is a case in point: it is as frightening and fascinating, as unfamiliar and attractive, as are many of the postindustrial sites around the world that

architects and developers have recently begun to reclaim.

RFG: **Describe your design proposal.**

PB: This is a very small garden for a designer who has an office in Basel and bought a weekend house in Sementina, in the canton of Ticino. The garden used to have fruit trees, palm trees, and camellias. We grouped the palms together, removed some of the fruit trees, and added some vines. Then we created a small access path to the side of the property, which connects to a lawn. In front of the garden is an inaccessible swamp, which is about 1,300 feet (400 meter) wide and several miles long, and beyond which is a river. For me, the relation between the garden and this landscape was more important than the garden itself. The design consists of a small terrace that touches the garden on one side and cantilevers over the landscape on the other sides, so that it is surrounded by wild

The terrace is hidden by the branches of trees and bushes. It becomes visible only gradually from the access path leading through the garden.

The Terrace on the Forest, seen through the trees

nature. I added two benches on the terrace in a way that permits maximum flexibility of use: you can sit on one of the benches and read a book, sit on the edge of the bench and put your elbows on the railing to look out at the view, add a small table and work with your laptop, or sit across from each other on the two opposite benches.

RFG: **How did you choose the exact position of the terrace?**

PB: The approach to the terrace is a very important part of my design. I wanted it to be a surprise. You don't see the terrace as you walk down the path, because it's hidden by the branches of ash trees, but you discover it suddenly at the very end, once you pass through the trees. I placed the terrace in front of a large existing tree. As you stand on the platform and look outward through the branches of the tree, it gives you an immense sense of depth.

RFG: **Did you consider using materials other than wood?**

PB: No, I wanted the structure to be light, because one of my concerns was that the design touch the soil only minimally. Concrete, for instance, would have been far too heavy. I wanted the terrace to float in the wilderness in order to accentuate the separation between nature and culture. I chose larch wood as the building material, because it is very resistant to water and the elements. We treated and painted it, and it has remained in very good condition.

RFG: **Is there anything that you would change today?**

PB: My client is very happy with his garden. He lives in the city, so when he comes to Sementina, he spends more time on the terrace than he does inside the house. I think this place gives you a

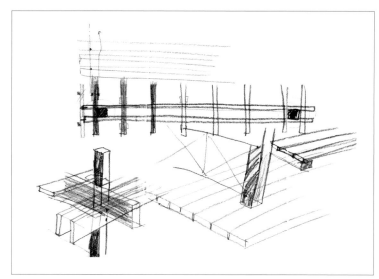
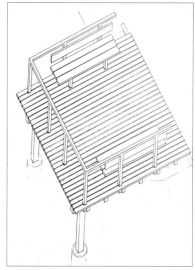

sense of peace. And it's great to know that nobody will destroy the landscape it looks out on by building something on it. No, I wouldn't change anything.

RFG: **In one of your essays you write that the appeal of many contemporary landscape projects is exhausted after the first glance. In a project like the Terrace on the Forest, which is so minimal, what keeps your client's interest alive?**

PB: I think it is important to design places that provide something for the spirit as well as for the senses. The terrace at Sementina is a peaceful place for contemplation, and contemplation can lead us to fantastic worlds, where there is room for playfulness, for poetry, and for dreams.

Think of the Sacro Bosco (Sacred Grove) at Bomarzo, twelve miles (nineteen kilometers) east of Viterbo, Italy. This five-hundred-year-old mannerist garden, designed by Vicino Orsini, has received a lot of attention since its creation. It's a fantastical place that offers the visitor an escape from the banality and ordinariness of the spaces of everyday life. Each sculptural group in the park is scattered along a winding path that leads visitors through a dense forest. And each "folly" is accompanied by puzzling inscriptions carved in stone. They inspire visitors with a sense of wonder, which arises from the presentation of the impossible under the appearance of verisimilitude. The sculptures and their mottoes present a combination of opposites intended to provoke astonishment and delight in visitors. A typical example is the famous tilted house that invites people to enter and make themselves at home, while its crazily tilted floors make anyone's stay there delightfully uneasy.

The mysteries of Bomarzo arouse emotions and make us think. They don't tire or bore us.

In order to achieve this, landscape architectural projects need to express human desires—and they can do this with very simple means—and invite the visitor to discover and interpret their message. This is what I hope I have achieved with the Terrace on the Forest.

The benches are designed for a variety of uses.

Something Behind the Horizon

John Dixon Hunt

There is prose and there is poetry in landscape architecture (and, of course, good and bad in both). There is absolutely nothing wrong with good prose: designs that accomplish the desired functions, like amenable paths, viewpoints, and benches where they are likely to be most useful; good and ecologically sound drainage; trash bins; handicap accessibility; planting that flourishes and enhances; interpretative labels; and so on. Prose generally sets itself a specific, definable task and tackles it with good grammar and, often, elegant syntax and vocabulary. Poetry is more difficult to define, a *je ne sais quoi* for both designer and visitor, but not at all negligible and generally recognizable. It is likely to extend the significance and experience of a designed place beyond those pragmatic necessities of good prose, though without neglecting, even if it challenges, the requisites of syntax and vocabulary. We may be tempted to say this "poetry" is about giving meaning to a site, but that risks isolating the

special quality in a verbal, discursive medium; poetry is not simply made of words, as Turner's watercolors or Bach's cantatas demonstrate. And yet, awkwardly and paradoxically, design critics are generally forced to express themselves verbally when they confront an exciting and poetic built work.

These broad distinctions may help when we confront work by Paolo Bürgi. Cardada, in the Ticinese mountains of Switzerland, may be by now something of a cliché in discussions of his work (like Duisberg for Peter Latz), but it is wonderfully rich and entirely representative of his skills at combining the prose and the poetry of design in landscape. We may parse them separately here: the prose of promenade, pathways and gathering areas; the factual orientations of panorama and geological reference; and the poetry of sublime experience, the thrust of pedestrians into thin air, the subtle recognitions of DNA and the mysterious workings of the physical world, the recognition of distant cataclysm. But these different registers (as linguists would say) overlap and shape each other. The poetry, if you like, emerges from the basic building blocks of Cardada's prose.

The physical elements of the site are accomplished with ease: the arrival platform at the top of the funicular, for instance, the woodland pathway that leads to the chair lift, or the basic amphitheater or stage of the geological observatory at the summit. Yet Bürgi has expanded each of these pragmatic spaces to incorporate further experiences. The floor of the arrival plaza is formed of granite chevrons that move outwards as the visitor enters the area, the space between them increasing and revealing more grass at each step; the effect is subtle, but announces our necessary movement into a more natural world. And the essential and wholly familiar experience of an alpine viewing platform that safely allows visitors to take in the view and click their camera shutters is augmented by the dizzy gesture of the walkway (the *promontorio paesaggistico*), which juts out over

the treetops and takes visitors seemingly right into the alpine sky. Bürgi has annotated this viewing platform with incised images of living organisms underfoot (a shrewd move, I think, if, like me, your reaction to walking out into nowhere is to fix your eyes on the available ground). The possible connections, the relevance or associations of these and other carvings on the ground and on the handrail, are not immediately apparent, so that the visitor will only gradually respond to the whole scenario (or what Bürgi himself terms a narrative).

This determination to embed signs of the site's history is much involved with Bürgi's emphasis upon process in landscape design. A tedious cliché in too much professional discourse, for him process emerges out of his profound response to the histories of a place, whether it be Helsinki, Cardada, or Kreuzlingen. We proceed, physically and imaginatively, into and through and beyond a physical site, and in Bürgi's view, it is the designer's job to put visitors in touch with its natural and cultural elements, to instigate a dialogue but not to control it (as would be the case with any literary narrative, in which a sequence is determined by both syntax and the *mise en page*). Bürgi's enthusiasm for the Fibonacci sequence, which is among the carvings at Cardada, is apt: the infinitely incremental extension of its arithmetic is a metaphor for our own potential involvement in understanding a place. Accustomed as I have been to walking in the mountains, it was at Cardada that I learned, not so much how intricate a landscape could be, but how a skillful organization of my visit by the designer inaugurated an intense involvement with a place, an involvement that, importantly, continued after leaving it.

Cardada's game path and the geological observatory both initiate stories, but leave us to make of them much more than they initially provide or provoke: a merry-go-round on the pathway introduces us to centrifugal force; a conventional diagram of surrounding peaks

attached to the observatory railing leads the eye to single out, on a distant hillside, the scar left ninety million years ago when the European and African plates slipped past each other. Detail, as Bürgi confesses, is everything to him, and he has an eye and an ear for the endless quiddities or "thingnesses" of the worlds into which he intervenes.

Our response to a place, especially a designed place, is (Bürgi argues) conditioned by our imagination and knowledge, by what we bring to it. Even good prose requires some attentive reading. But the poetry of design also requires some answering sensibility in its visitors, which, of course, the designer cannot anticipate at all precisely. This, I suspect, leads designers in three basic directions: toward heavy-handed, overtly prescriptive narrative, because they want to have an impact on visitors; or, because they realize the inherent impossibilities of anticipating an audience's responses, toward either banal functionality or self-important solipsism. That Bürgi escapes all those dead-ends of landscape design derives largely from his concern with place, with what used to be called "genius loci," though that phrase has lost its clout. Instead he emphasizes his search for the *essence* of a place. His seizing of essence, as his commentaries in this book reveal, is painstaking and complex, physical and metaphysical, looking and feeling, researching and responding. It is, I suggest, the depth or richness of those initial approaches to his sites that ensures that whatever Bürgi subsequently proposes as physical interventions are rich; that richness in turn becomes a complex resource for the imaginations and knowledge of a wide range of people to connect with it at one level or another.

One of Bürgi's favorite English expressions is "beautiful": students and colleagues hear it from him often, as adjective, but also as exclamation (and it recurs in his interview with Raffaella Fabiani Giannetto). It sometimes sounds a little funny, too limp and facile a verbal gesture in English. But I have always assumed that it is his translation (from which something has inevitably been lost) of *che bello!*, an Italian enunciation that rings more authentic, more attentive to the sudden apprehension of something striking and pleasing. Some landscape experiences are complex and dramatic, but others are simple and *sotto voce*. A truly great designer manages both. So there is Bürgi's fondness for simple fountains in the Cardada arrival plaza or at a local school courtyard, for concentric circles of trees outside a pharmaceutical headquarters, or for the little terrace at Sementina. When Bürgi took me to this private garden some years ago, he wanted me to go ahead of him and discover that the curving pathway leads onto a narrow platform, cantilevered over the gorge, with a pair of benches. From a design perspective it was but a small move, but it elicited a strong and lasting experience. *Che bello!*

Credits

**Cardada, Canton
Ticino, Switzerland**

CLIENT
Cardada Impianti Turistici,
Orselina, Switzerland

LANDSCAPE ARCHITECT
Paolo Bürgi

CONSTRUCTION
1999–2000

CONSULTANTS
Guido Maspoli,
Bellinzona (*biology*);
Giovanni Bertea,
Locarno (*history*);
Luca Bonzanigo,
Mario Codoni,
Markus Felber,
Paolo Oppizzi,
Canton Ticino (*geology*);
Flavio Paolucci,
Canton Ticino (*artist*)

**STRUCTURAL ENGINEERING,
VIEWING PLATFORM:**
Passera & Pedretti, Lugano

**STRUCTURAL ENGINEERING,
GEOLOGICAL OBSERVATORY:**
Stoffel Engineering, Locarno

PHOTOGRAPHERS
Giosanna Crivelli, Paolo Bürgi

COLLABORATION
Giorgio Aeberli

SKETCHES
Mei Wu

AWARDS
European Landscape Award Rosa
Barba, first prize, 2003

**Kreuzlingen Hafenplatz,
Canton Thurgau,
Switzerland**

CLIENT
Bauverwaltung (planning department) Kreuzlingen, Switzerland

LANDSCAPE ARCHITECT
Paolo Bürgi

CONSTRUCTION
2002–2003

CONSULTANTS
Planimpuls AG Civil Engineers,
Kreuzlingen

COLLABORATION
Sonja Dümpelmann, Giorgio
Aeberli

PHOTOGRAPHERS
Giosanna Crivelli, Paolo Bürgi

AWARDS
Swiss landscape award "Bronze
Hasenpreis die Besten" 2003

Terrace on the Forest,
Sementina, Canton
Ticino, Switzerland

CLIENT
private

LANDSCAPE ARCHITECT
Paolo Bürgi

CONSTRUCTION
1991

PHOTOGRAPHER
Paolo Bürgi

Bibliography

Asensio Cerver, Francisco Bahamón Alejandro. *Ultimate Landscape Design*. New York: teNeues, 2005.

Baldan Zenoni Politeo, Giuliana, and Pietrogrande Antonella. *Il Giardino e la memoria del mondo*. Firenze: L. S. Olschki, 2002.

"Bedeutsame Gärten / Gardens with Meanings." *Daidalos* 15, no. 46 (1992).

Bürgi, Paolo. "Vom Perimeter zum Horizont: Reale und Imaginäre Grenzen" (From the Perimeter to the Horizon: Real Limits—Imaginary Limits). *Topos: European Landscape Magazine* 50 (2005): 32–8.

———. "Memory and Imagination: History as a Source of Inspiration." In *Historic Gardens Today: To Commemorate the 80th Birthday of*

Professor Dr. Dieter Hennebo, eds. Michael Rohde and Rainer Schomann, 66–71. Leipzig, Germany: Edition Leipzig, 2004.

———. "Cardada: Gedanken über einen Berg" (Cardada: Reconsidering a Mountain). *Topos: European Landscape Magazine* 36 (2001): 6–12.

———. "Mysterium und Verwunderung" (Mystery and Wonder). *Topos: European Landscape Magazine* 19 (1997): 19–22.

———. "Eine Erinnerung an das Schöne" (A Recollection of Beauty). *Anthos* 34 (1995): 2–3.

———. "Die Entmystifizierung des Bodens" (Demystification of the Ground). *Anthos* 31 (1992): 2–3.

"Bürogarten von Paolo Bürgi in Camorino, Tessin" (Paolo Bürgi's Bureau Garden in Camorino, Ticino). *Anthos* 27 (1988): 8–9.

Cappelletti, Novella. "Alla Scoperta Dell'orizzonte" (Discovering the Horizon). *Ville giardini* 393 (2003): 80–3.

Cassatela, Claudia, and Francesca Bagliani. *Creare paesaggi : realizzazioni, teorie e progetti in europa: catalogo della rassegna e atti del convegno: la creazione di nuovi paesaggi* (Creating Landscapes: Designs, Theories, and Projects in Europe: Catalogue of the Exhibition and Conference Procedures: The Creation of New Landscapes). Firenze: Alinea, 2003.

Clouzot, Henri-Georges. "Le Mystère Picasso" (The Mystery of Picasso), video. 1956.

Davoine, Gilles. "Paolo Bürgi: Aménagements Paysagers En Montagne, Locarno-Cardada, Suisse." *Moniteur architecture AMC* 119 (2001): 100–[5].

Dixon-Hunt, John. "The Afterlife of Gardens." In *Penn Studies In Landscape Architecture*. Philadelphia: University of Pennsylvania Press, 2004.

Fieldwork: Landscape Architecture Europe. Triennial of Contemporary European Landscape Architecture. Wageningen, the Netherlands: LAE, 2006.

"Hafenplatz in Kreuzlingen" (Harbor Square in Kreuzlingen). *Architektur + Wettbewerbe* 200 (2004): 44–5.

Hauxner, Malene. *Open to the Sky: The Second Phase of the Modern Breakthrough 1950–1970:*

Building and Landscape, Spaces and Works, City Landscape. Copenhagen: Arkitektens Forlag, 2003.

Les Plus Beaux Jardins Et Parcs De Suisse (The Most Beautiful Gardens and Parcs of Switzerland). Zurich: Patrimoine suisse, 2006.

Moffat, David. "Cardada: Reconsidering a Mountain [Edra]." *Places* 15 (2002): 56–8.

Ponticelli, Loredana, and Cesare Micheletti. *Nuove Infrastrutture Per Nuovi Paesaggi* (New Infrastructure for New Landscapes). Milan: Skira, 2003.

Rappaport, Nina. "Infrastructure and Motion." *Van Alen Report* 15. New York: Van Alen Institute Projects in Public Architecture, 2003.

Reyes Ferreira, Jesús. *Homenaje a Chucho Reyes, Jesús Reyes Ferreira: Agosto-Octubre De 1984, Museo Rufino Tamayo, Arte Contemporáneo Internacional.* Mexico City: El Museo, 1984.

Ryan, Hugh. "The Only Way to Climb a Mountain." *Compass* 20 (2001/2): 13–15.

"Seeuferanlage Sisikon Ur" (Lakeside Facilities at Sisikon Ur). *Anthos* 30 (1991): 24–7.

Senner, Johann, Thomas Loacker, and Rudolf Lüthi. *Bodensee: Ein Begleiter zu Neuer Landschaftsarchitektur* (Lake Constance: A Guide to New Landscape Architecture). Edition Garten + Landschaft. Munich: Callwey, 2007.

Venturi Ferriolo, Massimo. "Cardada by Paolo Bürgi: The Experience of the Gaze." In *Contemporary Garden Aesthetics, Creations and Interpretations, Dumbarton Oaks Colloquium on the History of Landscape Architecture,* 29, ed. Michel Conan, 199–222. Cambridge, Mass.: Harvard University Press, 2007.

Zanco, Federica. *Luis Barragán: The Quiet Revolution.* 1st ed. Milan: Skira, 2001.

Biographies

RAFFAELLA FABIANI GIANNETTO is a landscape historian and critic. She received her Ph.D. from the University of Pennsylvania in 2004 and currently teaches design studios and landscape architectural history and theory at the Department of Plant Science and Landscape Architecture at the University of Maryland. In addition to maintaining an interest in contemporary landscape architecture, Fabiani Giannetto's research centers on the Italian Renaissance garden, its legacy and historiography. Her most recent publication is *Medici Gardens: From Making to Design* (University of Pennsylvania Press, 2008). She has lectured in Europe at the Studienkurs des Kunsthistorischen Instituts in Florence, Italy and at the 6th International Conference for Word and Image Studies in Hamburg, Germany, and in the United States at New School University in New York, at the University of Pennsylvania in Philadelphia, and at Dumbarton Oaks in Washington, D.C.

JOHN DIXON HUNT was professor of the history and theory of landscape at the University of Pennsylvania, and was chair of the Department of Landscape Architecture when Paolo Bürgi began to teach studio classes there. Hunt has written widely on gardens and landscape architecture. His most recent books are *The Afterlife of Gardens*, *Nature Over Again: The Garden Art of Ian Hamilton Finlay*, and *The Venetian City Garden: Place, Typology and Perception*. He is the editor of the monograph series Penn Studies in Landscape Architecture and of the journal *Studies in the History of Gardens and Designed Landscapes*.

SONJA DÜMPELMANN is assistant professor of landscape architecture at the University of Maryland, where she teaches design studios and courses in landscape architecture history. She received her Ph.D. from the Berlin University of the Arts, in 2002. She curated exhibitions in the field of landscape architecture history and worked in Paolo Bürgi's studio from 2002 to 2003. Her book on the landscape architect Maria Teresa Parpagliolo Shephard and landscape architecture in Fascist Italy was published in 2004. Amongst her most recent publications is an edited volume on Prince Hermann von Pückler-Muskau's reception in America. Her research interests include the history of gardens, parks, and landscapes, city and regional planning, cartography, and cross-cultural influences in design and design theory.